COMPLETE IN CHRIST

AND

LOVE'S LOGIC

COMPLETE IN CHRIST

AND

LOVE'S LOGIC

BY

C. H. SPURGEON

BAKER BOOK HOUSE
Grand Rapids, Michigan

Paperback edition issued 1978
by Baker Book House
from the edition issued in 1892
by Hodder & Stoughton, Inc.

ISBN: 0-8010-8130-0

PHOTOLITHOPRINTED BY CUSHING - MALLOY, INC.
ANN ARBOR, MICHIGAN, UNITED STATES OF AMERICA
1978

I

COMPLETE IN CHRIST

" Ye are complete in Him."—COL. ii. 10.

THE pardoned sinner for a while is
content with the one boon of forgiveness, and is too overjoyed with a
sense of freedom from bondage to know
a wish beyond. In a little time, however,
he bethinks himself of his position, his
wants, and his prospects: what is then
his rapture at the discovery that the roll
of his pardon is also an indenture of all
wealth, a charter of all privileges, a title-

deed of all needed blessings! Having received Christ, he hath obtained all things in Him. He looketh to that cross upon which the dreadful handwriting of ordinances hath been nailed; to his unutterable surprise he beholds it blossom with mercy, and like a tree of life bring forth the twelve manner of fruits—yea, all that he requires for life, for death, for time, or for eternity. Lo! at the foot of the once accursed tree grow plants for his healing, and flowers for his delight; from the bleeding feet of the Redeemer flows directing love to lead him all the desert through—from the pierced side there gushes cleansing water to purge him from the power of sin—the nails

become a means of securing him to righteousness, while above the crown hangs
visible as the gracious reward of perse-
verance. All things are in the cross—by
this we conquer, by this we live, by this
we are purified, by this we continue firm
to the end. While sitting beneath the
shadow of our Lord we think ourselves
most rich, for angels seem to sing, "Ye
are complete in Him."

"COMPLETE IN HIM!"—precious sentence! sweeter than honey to our soul,
we would adore the Holy Spirit for dic-
tating such glorious words to His servant
Paul. Oh! may we by grace be made
to see that they really are ours—for ours
they are if we answer to the character

described in the opening verses of the
Epistle to the Colossians. If we have
faith in Jesus Christ, love towards all the
saints, and a hope laid up in heaven, we
may grasp this golden sentence as all our
own. Reader, hast thou been able to
follow in that which has already been
described as the "way which leads from
banishment"? Then thou mayst take
this choice sentence to thyself as a portion
of thine inheritance; for weak, poor,
helpless, unworthy though thou be in
thyself, in *Him*, thy Lord, thy Redeemer
thou art complete in the fullest, broadest,
and most varied sense of that mighty
word, and thou wilt be glad to muse upon
the wonders of this glorious position.

May the great Teacher guide us into this mystery of the perfection of the elect in Jesus, and may our meditation be cheering and profitable to our spirits ! As the words are few, let us dwell on them, and endeavour to gain the sweets which lie so compactly within this little cell.

Pause over those two little words, " *in Him* "—in Christ ! Here is the doctrine of union and oneness with Jesus—a doctrine of undoubted truth and unmingled comfort. The Church is so allied with her Lord that she is positively one with Him. She is the bride, and He the bridegroom ; she is the branch, and He the stem ; she the body, and He the glorious head. So also is every individual believer united to Christ. As Levi lay in the loins of Abraham when Melchizedek met him, so was every believer chosen in Christ, and blessed with all spiritual blessings in heavenly places in Him. We have been spared, protected, converted, justified, and accepted solely and entirely by virtue of our eternal union with Christ.

Never can the convinced soul obtain peace until, like Ruth, she finds rest in the house of her kinsman, who becomes her husband—Jesus the Lord. An eminent pastor, lately deceased,* said in one of his sermons, " Now, I am as sure as I am of my own existence that wherever God

* Rev. Joseph Irons, Camberwell.

the Holy Ghost awakens the poor sinner by His mighty grace, and imparts spiritual life in his heart, nothing will ever satisfy that poor sinner but a believing assurance of eternal union with Christ. Unless the soul obtains a sweet and satisfactory consciousness of it in the exercise of a living faith, it will never 'enter into rest' this side eternity."

It is from oneness with Christ before all worlds that we receive all our mercies. Faith is the precious grace which discerns this eternal union, and cements it by another—a vital union; so that we become one, not merely in the eye of God, but in our own happy experience—one in aim, one in heart, one in holiness, one in communion, and, ultimately, one in glory.

This manifest union is not more real and actual than the eternal union of which it is the revelation; it does not commence the union, nor does its obscurity or clearness in the least affect the certainty or safety of the immutable oneness subsisting between Jesus and the believer. It is eminently desirable that every saint should attain a full assurance of his union to Christ, and it is exceedingly important that he should labour to maintain a constant sense thereof; for although the mercy be the same, yet his comfort from it will vary according to his apprehension of it. A landscape is as fair by night as by day, but who can perceive its beauties in the dark?—even so we must see, or rather believe, this union to rejoice in it.

No condition out of Paradise can be more blessed than that which is produced by a lively sense of oneness with Jesus. To know and feel that our interests are mutual, our bonds indissoluble, and our lives united, is indeed to dip our morsel in the golden dish of heaven. There is no sweeter canticle for mortal lips than the sweet song, " My Beloved is mine, and I am His,"—

" E'en like two bank-dividing brooks,
  That wash the pebbles with their wanton streams,

And, having rang'd and search'd a thousand
    nooks,
Meet both at length in silver-breasted Thames,
Where in a greater current they conjoin ;—
So I my best Beloved's am, so He is mine."

Verily the stream of life floweth along
easily enough when it is commingled with
Him who is our life. Walking with our
arm upon the shoulder of the Beloved is
not simply safe, but delightful ; and
living with His life is a noble style of
immortality, which may be enjoyed on
earth. But to be out of Christ is misery,
weakness, and death—in short, it is the
bud, of which the full-blown flower is
damnation. Apart from Jesus we have
nothing save fearful forebodings and

terrible remembrances. Beloved, there is no Gospel promise which is ours unless we know what it is to be *in Him*. Out of Him all is poverty, woe, sorrow, and destruction : it is only in Him, the ark of His elect, that we can hope to enjoy covenant mercies, or rejoice in the sure blessings of salvation. Can we now entertain a hope that we are really hidden in the rock ? Do we feel that we are a portion of Christ's body, and that a real union exists between us ? Then may we proceed to unfold and appropriate the privileges here mentioned.

Ye are *complete* in Him. The word "complete" does not convey the whole of the meaning couched in the original word πεπληρωμένοι. It is upon the whole the best word which can be found in our language, but its meaning may be further unveiled by the addition of other auxiliary readings.

I. Ye are complete in Him. Let us consider the meaning of the phrase as it thus stands in our own Authorised Version. We are *complete*. In all matters which concern our spiritual welfare, and our soul's salvation, we are complete in Christ.

1. *Complete without the aid of Jewish ceremonies.* These had their uses. They were pictures wherewith the law, as a schoolmaster, taught the infant Jewish

church ; but now that faith is come, we are no longer under a schoolmaster, for in the clear light of Christian knowledge we need not the aid of symbols :—

"Finished are the types and shadows
Of the ceremonial law."

The one sacrifice has so atoned for us that we need no other. In Christ we are complete without any addition of circumcision, sacrifice, passover, or temple service. These are now but beggarly elements. They would be incumbrances— for what can we need from them when we are complete in Christ? What have we to do with moon or stars, now that Christ hath shone forth like the sun in his strength? Let the dim lamps be quenched—they would but mock the dawn, and the sunlight would deride their unneeded glimmerings. We despise not the ceremonial law—it was "the shadow of good things to come," and as such we venerate it; but now that the substance hath appeared, we are not content with guesses of grace, but we grasp Him who is grace and truth. How much more highly are we favoured than the ancient believers, for they by daily offerings confessed themselves to be incomplete! They could never stay their hand and say, "It is enough," for daily sin demanded daily lambs for the altar. The Jews were never made complete by their law, for their rites "could never make the comers thereunto perfect;" but this is our peculiar and superior privilege, that we are perfected by the one offering on Calvary.

2. *We are complete without the help of philosophy.* In Paul's time there were some who thought that philosophy might be used as a supplement to faith. They argued, contended, and mystified every doctrine of revelation. Happy would it have been for them and the Church had they heeded the words of Paul, and kept entirely to the simplicity of the Gospel, glorying only in the cross of Christ! The Christian has such a sublime system of doctrine that he never need to fear the vain speculations of an

infidel science, nor need he ever call in
the sophisms of the worldly wise to
prop his faith—in Christ he is complete.
We have never heard of a dying believer
asking the aid of a worldly philosophy
to give him words of comfort in the hour
of dissolution. No! he has enough in
his own religion—enough in the person
of his Redeemer—enough in the com-
forts of the Holy Ghost. Never let us
turn aside from the faith because of the
sneer of the learned : this a Christian will
not, cannot do—for we see *that* eternal
evidence in our religion which we may
call its best proof, namely, the fact that
in it we are complete.

No man can add anything to the religion of Jesus. All that is consistent with truth is already incorporated in it, and with that which is not true it can form no alliance. There is nothing new in theology save that which is false. Those who seek to improve the Gospel of Jesus do but deface it. It is so perfect in itself that all additions to it are but excrescences of error ; and it renders us so complete that aught we join with it is supererogation, or worse than that. David would not go to the fight in Saul's armour, for he had not proved it ; so can we say, " The sling and stone are to us abundant weapons ; as for the mail of philosophy, we leave that for proud Goliaths to wear." One of the most evil signs of our day is its tendency to rationalism, spiritualism, and multitudes of other means of beclouding the simple faith of our Lord Jesus; but the Lord's chosen family will not be beguiled from their steadfastness, which is the only hope of an heretical generation; for they know whom they have believed, and will not renounce their confidence in Him for the sophistries of " the wise and prudent."

3. *Complete without the inventions of superstition.* God is the Author of all revealed and spiritual religion; but man would write an appendix. There must be works of supererogation, deeds of penance, acts of mortification, or else the poor papist can never be perfected.

Yea, when he has most vigorously applied the whip, when he has fasted even to physical exhaustion, when he has forfeited all that is natural to man—yet he is never sure that he has done enough, he can never say that he is complete; but the Christian, without any of these, feels that he has gained a consummation by those last words of his Saviour—" It is finished!" The blood of his agonising Lord is his only and all-sufficient trust. He despises alike the absolutions and the indulgences of priest or pontiff; he tramples on the refuge of lies which the deceiver has builded—his glory and boast ever centring in the fact that he is *complete in Christ.* Let but this sentence be preached throughout the earth, and believed by the inhabitants thereof, and all the despots on its surface could not buttress the tottering Church of Rome, even for a single hour. Men would soon cry out, "Away with the usurper! away with her pretensions! There is all in Christ; and what can she add thereto, saving her mummeries, pollutions, and corrupt abominations?"

4. *We are complete without human merit, our own works being regarded as filthy rags.* How many there are who, while waxing warm against popery, are fostering its principles in their own minds! The very marrow of popery is reliance on our own works; and in God's

sight the formalist and legalist are as contemptible, if found in an orthodox church, as if they were open followers of Antichrist. Brethren, let us see to it that we are resting alone in the righteousness of Jesus, that He is all in all to us. Let us never forget that if we are perfect in Him, we are perfect only in Him. While we would diligently cultivate works of holiness, let us be careful lest we seek to add to the perfect work of Jesus. The robe of righteousness that nature spins and weavers is too frail a fabric to endure the breath of the Almighty ; we must, therefore, cast it all away—creature doings must not be united with, or regarded as auxiliary to, divine satisfaction.

We would be holy, even as God is, but we are still confident that this will not be supplementing the great righteousness which is ours by imputation. No; though compassed with sin and surrounded by our depravity, we know that we are so complete in Jesus that we could not be more so, even were we free from all these things, and glorified as the spirits of just men made perfect.

Blessed completely through the God-man, let our unbelief be ashamed, and let our admiration be fastened upon this interesting and delightful state of privilege. Arise, believer! and behold thyself " perfect in Christ Jesus." Let not thy sins shake thy faith in the all-sufficiency of Jesus. Thou art, with all thy depravity, still in Him, and therefore complete. Thou hast need of nothing beyond what there is in Him. In Him thou art at this moment just, in Him entirely clean, in Him an object of divine approval and eternal love. *Now*, as thou art, and where thou art, thou art still complete. Feeble, forgetful, frail, fearful, and fickle in thyself, yet *in Him* thou art all that can be desired. Thine unrighteousness is covered, thy righteousness is accepted, thy strength is perfected, thy safety secured, and thy heaven certain. Rejoice, then, that thou art " complete in Him." Look on thine own nothingness and be humble, but look at Jesus, thy great Representative, and be glad.   Be not so intent upon thine own corruptions as to forget His immaculate purity, which He has given to thee.   Be not so mindful of thine original poverty as to forget the infinite riches which He has conferred upon thee. It will save thee many pangs if thou wilt learn to think of thyself as being *in Him*, and as being by His glorious grace accepted in Him, and perfect in Christ Jesus.

II. YE ARE FULLY SUPPLIED IN HIM. Having Him, we have all that we can possibly require.   The man of God is thoroughly furnished in the possession of his great Saviour.   He never need to

look for anything beyond, for in Him all
is treasured. Do we need *forgiveness* for
the past? Pardons, rich and free, are
with Jesus. Grace to cover all our sin
is there; grace to rise above our follies
and our faults. Is it *wisdom* which we
lack? He is made of God unto us
wisdom. His finger shall point out our
path in the desert; His rod and staff
shall keep us in the way when we walk
through the valley of the shadow of death.
In our combats with the foe do we feel
want of *strength*? Is He not Jehovah,
mighty to save? Will He not increase
power unto the faint, and succour the
fallen? Need we go to Assyria, or stay
on Egypt, for help? Nay, these are

broken reeds. Surely, in the Lord Jehovah have we righteousness and strength. The battle is before us, but we tremble not at the foe ; we feel armed at all points, clad in impenetrable mail, for we are fully supplied in Him. Do we deplore our ignorance ? He will give us *knowledge ;* He can open our ear to listen to mysteries unknown. Even babes shall learn the wonders of His grace, and children shall be taught of the Lord. No other teacher is required ; He is alone efficient and all-sufficient. Are we at times distressed ? We need not inquire for *comfort*, for in Him, the consolation of Israel, there are fats full of the oil of joy, and rivers of the wine of thanksgiving. The *pleasures* of the world are void to us, for we have infinitely more joy than they can give in *Him* who has made us complete.

Ah! my reader, whatever exigencies may arise, we shall never need to say, "We have searched, but cannot find what we require; for it is, and ever shall be, found in the storehouse of mercy, even in Jesus Christ." "It hath pleased the Father that in Him should *all* fulness dwell;" and truly none of the saints have ever complained of any failure in Him. Tens of thousands of them have drawn from this sacred well, yet is it as full as ever, and all who come to it are supplied with the full measure of their necessities. Jesus is not one single sprig of myrrh, but "*a bundle* of myrrh is my Beloved unto me ; "* not one mercy, but a string of mercies, for "my Beloved is unto me as *a cluster* of camphire." "In Christ is a cluster of all spiritual blessings ; all the blessings of the everlasting covenant are in His hands and at His disposal ; and saints are blessed with all spiritual blessings in heavenly places in Him. He is the believer's wisdom, righteousness, sanctification, and redemption. There is not a mercy we want but is in Him, or a blessing we enjoy but what we have received from Him. He is the believer's '*all in all.*' "† The word translated

---

* Sol. Song i. 13, 14. † Dr. Gill.

"complete" is used by Demosthenes in describing a ship as fully manned—and truly the Christian's ship, from prow to stern, is well manned by her Captain, who Himself steers the vessel, stills the storm, feeds the crew, fills the sails, and brings all safe to their desired haven. In every position of danger or duty Christ Himself is all-sufficient for protection or support. Under every conceivable or inconceivable trial, we shall find in Him sufficient grace : should every earthly stream be dried, there is enough in Him, in the absence of them all. His glorious person is the dwelling-place of all-sufficiency. "In Him dwelleth all the fulness of the Godhead bodily ; " as the fulness of Deity is sufficient to create and sustain a universe of ponderous orbs, and whole worlds of living creatures, can it be supposed that it will be found unable to supply the necessities of saints ? Such a fear would be as foolish as if a man should tremble lest the atmosphere should prove too little for his breath, or the rivers too shallow for his thirst. To imagine the riches of the incarnate God to fail would be to conceive a bankrupt God, or a wasted infinite. Therefore, let us set up our banners in His name, and exceedingly rejoice.

III. A third reading is—YE ARE SATIS-FIED IN HIM. Satisfaction is a jewel rare and precious. Happy is the merchantman who finds it. We may seek it in *riches*, but it lieth not there. We may heap up gold and silver, pile on pile, until we are rich beyond the dream of avarice, then thrust our hands into our bags of gold, and search there for satisfaction, but we have it not. Our heart, like the horse-leech, crieth, " Give, give ! " We may erect the palace and conquer mighty nations, but among the trophies which decorate the hall, there is not that precious thing which worlds cannot buy. But give us Christ, let us be allied to Him, and our heart is satisfied. We are content in poverty—we are rich ; in distress we have all, and abound. We are full, for we are satisfied in Him.

Again, let us explore the fields of *know-ledge ;* let us separate ourselves, and intermeddle with all wisdom ; let us dive into the secrets of nature ; let the heavens yield to the telescope, and the earth to our research ; let us turn the ponderous tome, and pore over the pages of the mighty folio ; let us take our seat among the wise, and become professors of science ; but, alas ! we soon shall loathe it all, for "much study is a weariness of the flesh." But let us turn again to the fountain-head, and drink of the waters of revelation : we are then satisfied. What-ever the pursuit may be, whether we invoke the trump of fame to do us homage, and bid our fellows offer the

incense of honour, or pursue the pleasures of sin, and dance a giddy round
of merriment, or follow the less erratic
movements of commerce, and acquire
influence among men, we shall still be
disappointed, we shall have still an aching
void, an emptiness within; but when we
gather up our straying desires, and bring
them to a focus at the foot of Calvary,
we feel a solid satisfaction, of which the
world cannot deprive us.

Among the sons of men there are not
a few of restless spirit, whose uneasy
souls are panting for an unknown good,
the want of which they feel, but the
nature of which they do not comprehend.
These will hurry from country to country,

to do little else but attempt a hopeless escape from themselves; they will flit from pleasure to pleasure, with the only gain of fresh grief from repeated disappointments. It were hard indeed to compound a medicine for minds thus diseased. Verily, the aromatics and balms of Araby, or the islands of the sea, might be exhausted ere the elixir of satisfaction could be distilled, and every mystic name in the vocabulary of the wise might be tried in vain to produce the all-precious charm of quiet. But in the Gospel we find the inestimable medicine already compounded, potent enough to allay the most burning fever, and still the most violent palpitations of the heart. This we speak from experience, for we too were once, like the unclean spirit, "seeking rest and finding none;" we once groaned for an unseen something, which in all our joys we could not find, and now, by God's great love, we have found the water which has quenched our thirst—it is that which Jesus gives, "the living water" of His grace. We revel in the sweets of the name of Jesus, and long for nought beside. Like Naphtali, we are satisfied with favour, and full of the blessing of the Lord. Like Jacob, we exclaim, "It is enough." The soul is anchored, the desire is "satiated with fatness," the whole man is rich to all the intents of bliss, and looketh for nothing more. Allen, in his " Heaven Opened," represents the believer as soliloquising in the following joyous manner :—" O happy soul, how rich art thou ! What a booty have I gotten ! It is all mine own. I have the promises of this life and of that which is to come. Oh ! what can I wish more ? How full a charter is here ! Now, my doubting soul may boldly and believingly say with Thomas, ' My Lord and my God.' What need we any further witness ? We have heard His words. He hath sworn by His holiness that His decree may not be changed, and hath signed it with His own signet. And now return to thy rest, O my soul !

for the Lord hath dealt bountifully with thee. Say, if thy lines ·be not fallen to thee in a pleasant place, and if this be not a goodly heritage? O blasphemous discontent! how absurd and unreasonable an evil art thou, whom all the fulness of the Godhead cannot satisfy, because thou art denied in a petty comfort, or crossed in thy vain expectations from the world! O my unthankful soul, shall not a Trinity content thee? Shall not all-sufficiency suffice thee? Silence, ye murmuring thoughts, for ever. I have enough, I abound, and am full. Infiniteness and eternity are mine, and what more can I ask?"

Oh may we constantly dwell on the

blissful summit of spiritual content, boasting continually in the completeness of our salvation IN HIM, and may we ever seek to live up to our great and inestimable privilege ! Let us live according to our rank and quality, according to the riches conveyed to us by the eternal covenant. As great princes are so arrayed that you can read their estates in their garments, and discern their riches by their tables, so let our daily carriage express to others the value which we set upon the blessings of grace. A murmur is a rag which is ill-suited to be the dress of a soul possessed of Jesus; a complaining spirit is too mean a thing for an heir of all things to indulge. Let worldlings see that our

Jesus is indeed a sufficient portion. As for those of us who are continually filled with rejoicing, let us be careful that our company and converse are in keeping with our high position. Let our satisfaction with Christ beget in us a spirit too noble to stoop to the base deeds of ungodly men. Let us live among the generation of the just; let us dwell in the courts of the great King, behold His face, wait at His throne, bear His name, show forth His virtues, set forth His praises, advance His honour, uphold His interest, and reflect His image. It is not becoming that princes of the blood should herd with beggars, or dress as they do; let all believers, then, come out from the world,

and mount the hills of high and holy
living ; so shall it be proved that they are
content with Christ, when they utterly
forsake the broken cisterns.

IV. The text bears within it another
meaning—YE ARE FILLED IN HIM :—so
Wickliffe translated it, " 𝔞𝔫𝔡 𝔷𝔢 𝔟𝔢𝔫 𝔣𝔦𝔩𝔩𝔦𝔡
𝔦𝔫 𝔥𝔶𝔪." A possession of Jesus in the
soul is a filling thing. Our great Creator
never intended that the heart should be
empty, and hence He has stamped upon
it the ancient rule that nature abhors a
vacuum. The soul can never be quiet
until in every part it is fully occupied.
It is as insatiable as the grave, until it
finds every corner of its being filled

with treasure. Now, it can be said of Christian salvation, that it, and it alone, can fill the mind. Man is a compound being, and while one portion of his being may be full, another may be empty. There is nothing which can fill the whole man save the possession of Christ.

The man of hard calculation, the lover of facts, may feast his head and starve his heart;—the sentimentalist may fill up his full measure of emotion, and destroy his understanding;—the poet may render his imagination gigantic, and dwarf his judgment;—the student may render his brain the very refinement of logic, and his conscience may be dying:—but give us Christ for our study, Christ for our science, Christ for our pursuit, and our whole man is filled. In His religion we find enough to exercise the faculties of the most astute reasoner, while yet our heart, by the contemplation, shall be warmed—yea, made to burn within us. In Him we find room for imagination's utmost stretch, while yet His kind hand preserves us from wild and romantic visions. He can satisfy our soul in its every part. Our whole man feels that His truth is our soul's proper food, that its powers were made to appropriate *Him*, while *He* is so constituted that He is adapted to its every want. Herein lies the fault of all human systems of religion

—they do but subjugate and enlist a portion of the man; they light up with doubtful brilliance one single chamber of his soul, and leave the rest in darkness; they cover him in one part, and allow the biting frost to benumb and freeze the other, until the man feels that something is neglected, for he bears a gnawing within him which his false religion cannot satisfy. But let the glorious Gospel of the blessed Jesus come into the man; let the Holy Spirit apply the word with power, and the whole man is filled—every nerve, like the string of a harp, is wound up, and gives forth melody—every power blesses God—every portion is lighted up with splendour, and the man exclaims,—

"There rest, my long divided soul,
 Fixed on this mighty centre, rest."

"Shaddai," the Lord all-sufficient, is a portion large enough to afford us fulness of joy and peace. In Him, as well as in His house, "there is bread enough and to spare." In the absence of all other good things, He is an overflowing river of mercy, and when other blessings are present, they owe all their value to Him. He makes our cup so full that it runneth over, and so He is just what man's insatiable heart requires. It is a fact which all men must acknowledge, that we are never full till we run over—the soul never has enough till it has more than enough; while we can contain and measure and number our possessions, we are not quite so rich as we desire. *Pauperis est numerare pecus*—we count ourselves poor so long as we can count our wealth. We are never satisfied till we have more than will satisfy us. But in Jesus there is that superabundance, that lavish richness, that outdoing of desire, that we are obliged to exclaim, "*It is enough—I m filled to the brim.*"

How desirable is that state of mind which makes every part of the soul a spring of joys! The most of men have but one well of mirth within them; according to their temperament, they derive their happiness from different powers of the mind—one from bold imagination, another from solitary meditation, and a third from memory; but the believer has many wells and many palm-trees, for all that is within him is blessed by God. As the waters cover the sea, so has divine grace flooded every portion of his being. He has no "aching void," no "salt land, and not inhabited," no "clouds without rain;" but where once were disappointment and discontent, there are now "pleasures for evermore," for the soul is "filled in Him."

Seek then, beloved Christian reader, to know more and more of Jesus. Think not that thou art master of the science of Christ crucified. Thou knowest enough of Him to be supremely blest; but thou art even now but at the beginning. Notwithstanding all thou hast learned of Him, remember thou hast but read the child's first primer; thou art as yet on one of the lower forms; thou hast not yet a degree in the sacred college. Thou hast but dipped the sole of thy foot in that stream wherein the glorified are now swimming. Thou art but a gleaner—thou hast not at present handled the sheaves with which the ransomed returned to Zion. King Jesus hath not showed thee *all* the treasures of His house, nor canst thou more than guess the value of the least of His jewels. Thou hast at this moment a very faint idea of the glory to which thy Redeemer has raised thee, or the completeness with which He has enriched thee. Thy joys are but sips of the cup, but crumbs from under the table. Up then to thine inheritance, the land is before thee, walk through and survey the lot of thine inheritance; but this know, that until thou hast washed in Jordan, thou shalt be but as a beginner, not only in the whole science of divine love, but even in this one short but comprehensive lesson: "COMPLETE IN HIM."

TO THE UNCONVERTED READER.

FRIEND,—We will venture one assertion, in the full belief that thou canst not deny it—*thou art not entirely satisfied*. Thou art one of the weary-footed seekers of a joy which thou wilt never find out of Christ. Oh! let this chapter teach thee to forgo thy vain pursuit, and look in another direction. Be assured that, as hitherto thy chase has been a disappointment, so shall it continue to the end, unless thou dost run in another manner. Others have digged the mines of worldly pleasure, and have gained nothing but anguish and despair; wilt thou search again where others have found nothing? Let the experience of ages teach thee the fallacy of human hopes, and let thine own failures warn thee of new attempts.

But hark! sinner, all thou needest is in

Christ. He will fill thee, satisfy thee, enrich thee, gladden thee. Oh ! let thy friend beseech thee, " Taste and see that the Lord is good."

II

LOVE'S LOGIC

II

LOVE'S LOGIC

" The upright love Thee."—Song of Solomon 1. 4.

THE motives of love are in a great
degree the measure of its growth.
The advanced believer loves his Lord for
higher reasons than those which move
the heart of the young convert. His
affection is not more sincere or earnest,
but it is, or ought to be, more steadfast
and unvarying, because experience has
enabled the understanding to adduce
more abundant reasons for the soul's

attachment.   All true love to the Redeemer is acceptable to Him, and is to
us an infallible evidence of our safety in
Him.   We are far from depreciating the
value or suspecting the sincerity of the
warm emotions of the newly enlightened,
although we prefer the more intelligent
and less interested attachment of the well-
instructed Christian.   Let none doubt
the reality of their piety because they are
unable to mount to all the heights, or
dive into all the depths, of that love
which passeth knowledge.   A babe's
fondness of its mother is as pleasing to
her as the strong devotion of her full-
grown son.   The graces of faith, hope,
and love are to be estimated more by

their honesty than by their degree, and less by their intellectual than by their emotional characteristics. Yet, without doubt, growth in grace is as much displayed in the Christian's love as in any other fruit of the Spirit; and it is our belief that this growth may in some degree be traced by the motives which cause it, just as we trace the motion of the shower by the position of the cloud from which it falls. It may be profitable to dwell upon the motives of love for a brief season, hoping for instruction in so doing. We do not pretend to enter fully into the present subject; and, indeed, our space prevents us as much as our incapacity. Owen's remark will be appropriate here

" Motives unto the love of Christ are so great, so many, so diffused through the whole dispensation of God in Him unto us, as that they can by no hand be fully expressed, let it be allowed ever so much to enlarge in the declaration of them ; much less can they be represented in this short discourse, whereof but a very small part is allotted unto their consideration." *

In enumerating some of the stages of spiritual growth as indicated by higher standards of motive, we pray the Holy Spirit to guide our meditations, giving us profitable wisdom and gracious enlightenment. Let us commence in entire de-

* " Christologia."

pendence upon His aid, and so proceed from step to step as He shall be pleased to guide us. We commence with the Alpha of Love, the first ripe fruit of affection.

I. LOVE OF GRATITUDE. "We love Him because He first loved us." Here is the starting-point of love's race. This is the rippling rill which afterwards swells into a river, the torch with which the pile of piety is kindled. The emancipated spirit loves the Saviour for the freedom which He has conferred upon it; it beholds the agony with which the priceless gift was purchased, and it adores the bleeding Sufferer for the pains which He so generously endured. Jesus is regarded as our Benefactor, and the boons which we receive at His hands constrain us to give Him our hearts. If enabled to receive all the doctrines of the Gospel, we bless the name of our Redeemer for His free grace manifested in our election to eternal life ; for His efficacious grace exercised in calling us into His kingdom ; for pardon and justification through His blood and merits, and for everlasting security by virtue of union with His divine Person. Surely here is enough to create love of the highest order of fervency ; and if the soul should abide for ever in contemplation of these mighty acts of grace, without entering upon the glorious survey of the character and perfections of Jesus, it need never be in want of reasons for affection. Here are coals enough to maintain the heavenly fire, if the Holy Spirit be but present to fan the flame. This order of affection is capable of producing the most eminent virtues, and stimulating the most ardent zeal. It is enough for every practical purpose of the heavenly life. But, nevertheless, there is a " yet beyond." There are other motives which are of a higher class in themselves, although very seldom more potent in their influence. This, however, is the beginning "I love the Lord because He has heard my voice and my supplication." It is His kindness toward us, rather than the graciousness of His nature which primarily attracts us.

The deeds of the Saviour do not so much arouse our early admiration from their intrinsic greatness and graciousness, as from the fact that *we* have a share in them. This thought at first attracts all our regard, and engrosses all our meditations. Neither the person nor the offices of Christ have as yet been fully presented to the soul,—it knows Him only in His gifts, and loves Him only for what He has bestowed. Call this love selfish if you will, but do not condemn it. The Saviour frowned not on the woman who loved much, because much had been forgiven, nor did He despise the offering of that heart which was first moved with affection at the casting out of its seven devils. Perhaps it is from a selfish reason that the infant casts the tendrils of its heart around its mother, but who would therefore despise its fondness? Base must be the man who should wish to eradicate such a heavenly germ because of the poverty of the soil in which it grew. Our love to God may even be heightened by due and wise self-love. "There is a *sinful* self-love, when either we love that for a self which is not ourself,—when we love our flesh and fleshly interest,—or when we love ourselves inordinately, more than God, and God only for ourselves; and there is a *lawful* self-love, when we love ourselves *in the Lord and for the Lord.*" * This lawful self-love leads us to love Christ, and to desire more and more of His grace, because we feel that so we shall be the more happy in our souls, and useful in our lives. This is in some degree earthy, but in no degree sinful, or anything but holy.

It is not needful that the foundation-stones should be of polished marble, they will well enough subserve their purpose if they act as the underlying groundwork of more excellent materials. If it be a crime to be ungrateful, then thankfulness is a virtue, and its issue cannot be con-

---

* Allen's " Riches of the Covenant."

temptible. Young beginners frequently
doubt their piety, because they feel but
little disinterested affection for the Lord
Jesus ; let them remember that that high
and excellent gift is not one of the tender
grapes, but is only to be gathered beneath
the ripening skies of Christian experience.
" Do you love Christ ? " is the important
question, and if the answer be a firm
avowal of attachment to Him, it is deci-
sive as to your spiritual condition, even
though the further question, " Why do
you love Him ? " should only receive
for answer, " I love Him because He
first loved me." Indeed, in the loftiest
stage of heavenly life there must ever be
a great and grateful mixture of motives

in our love to our divine Master. We
do not cease to love Him for His mercies
when we begin to adore Him for His
personal excellencies; on the contrary,
our sense of the glory of the Person
who is our Redeemer increases our
gratitude to Him for His condescending
regard of such insignificant creatures as
ourselves. Thus the ripening shock of
corn can hold fellowship with the tender
blade, since both are debtors to the sun-
shine. Even the saints before the throne
are in no small degree moved to rapturous love of their exalted King, by the
very motive which some have been ready
to undervalue as selfish and unspiritual.
They sing, "Thou art worthy, for Thou

wast slain, and *hast redeemed us* unto God by Thy blood ; " and in their song who shall ever doubt that grace, free grace, as exhibited in their own salvation, holds the highest place.

Oh, new-born soul, trembling with anxiety, if thou hast not yet beheld the fair face of thy Beloved, if thou canst not as yet delight in the majesty of His offices, and the wonders of His person, let thy soul be fully alive to the richness of His grace and the precious-ness of His blood. These thou hast in thy possession,—the pledges of thine interest in Him ; love Him then for these, and in due time He will dis-cover unto thee fresh wonders and glories, so that thou shalt be able to exclaim, "The half has not been told me." Let Calvary and Gethsemane endear thy Saviour to thee, though as yet thou hast not seen the brightness of Tabor, or heard the eloquence of Olivet. Take the lower room if thou canst not reach another, for *the lowest room is in the house*, and its tables shall not be naked. But study to look into thy Redeemer's heart, that thou mayest become more closely knit unto Him. Remember there is a singular love in the bowels of our Lord Jesus to His people, so superlatively excellent, that nothing can compare with it. No husband, no wife, nor tender-hearted mother can compete with Him in affection, for His love passeth the love of women. Nothing will contribute more to make thee see Jesus Christ as admirable and lovely than a right apprehension of His love to thee : this is the constraining, ravishing, engaging, and overwhelming consideration which will infallibly steep thee in a sea of love to Him. "Although," says Durham,* "there be much in many mouths of Christ's love, yet there are few that really know and believe the love that He hath to His people. (1 John iii. 1.) As this is the cause that so few love Him, and why so many set up other beloveds beside Him, so the solid

---

* "Exposition of Sol. Song."

faith of this and the expectation of good
from Him, hath a great engaging virtue
to draw sinners to Him." Study then
His love, and so inflame thine own; for
be thou ever mindful that the love of
Jesus was costly on His part, and un-
deserved on thine.

Here it will be right to mention the
love which springs from a sense of *pos-*
session of Christ. "O Lord, *Thou art*
my God, early will I seek Thee," is the
vow which results from a knowledge of
our possessing God as our own. As God
we *ought* to love Him, but as *our* God
we *do* love Him. It is Christ as *our*
Christ, His righteousness as imputed to
us, and His atonement as *our* ransom.

which at first cause our souls to feel the heat of love. "I cannot love another man's Christ," saith the anxious soul. "He must be mine, or my soul can never be knit unto Him ; " but when an interest in Jesus is perceived by the understanding, then the heart cries out, "My Lord and my God, Thou art mine, and I will be Thine." It is worth while to be a man, despite all the sorrows of mortality, if we may have grace to talk in the fashion of a full assured believer, when he rejoices in the plenitude of his possessions, and gratefully returns his love as his only possible acknowledgment. Listen to him while he talks in the following strains :—
" *My* Beloved is mine, and I am His.

The grant is clear, and my claim is firm. Who shall despoil me of it when God hath put me in possession, and doth own me as the lawful heritor? *My* Lord hath Himself assured me that He is mine, and hath bid me call His Father, *my* father. I know of a surety that the whole Trinity are *mine*. 'I will be *thy* God' is my sweet assurance. O my soul, arise and take possession; inherit thy blessedness, and cast up thy riches; enter into *thy* rest, and tell how the Lord hath dealt bountifully with thee. I will praise Thee, O *my* God; *my* King, I subject my soul unto Thee. O *my* Glory, in Thee will I boast all the day; O *my* Rock, on Thee will I build all my confidence. O staff of my life and strength of my heart, the life of my joy and joy of my life, I will sit and sing under Thy shadow, yea, I will sing a song of loves touching my WELL-BELOVED." This is a precious experience ; happy is the man who enjoys it. It is the marrow of life to read our title clear ; and it is so for this reason, among others, that it creates and fosters a devout ardency of affection in the soul which is the possessor of it. Let all believers seek after it.

II. Akin to the love inspired by thankfulness, but rising a step higher in gracious attainments, is LOVE CAUSED BY ADMIRATION *of the manner in which the work of the Redeemer was performed.* Having loved Him for the deed of salvation, the believer surveys the labours of his Deliverer, and finds them in every part so excellent and marvellous, that he loves Him with new force as he meditates upon them. HE is altogether lovely to the soul in every office which HE was graciously pleased to assume. We behold Him as *our King,* and when we see the power, the justice, and the grace which attend His throne, when we witness the conquest of His enemies, and remark His strong defence of His friends, we cannot but adore Him, and exclaim, " All hail, we crown Thee Lord of all." If His *priestly* office engages our meditation, it is precious to view Him as the faithful High Priest; remembering the efficacy of His mediation; and the prevalence of His intercession: or, if the mantle of the *prophet* is viewed as worn by Him upon whose brow the crown of empire and the diadem of the priesthood are both for ever placed, how becoming does it seem upon His shoulders who is wisdom's self! In His threefold character, in which all the offices are blended, but none confused—all fulfilled, but none neglected —all carried to their highest length, but none misused,—how glorious does our Redeemer appear! Sonnets will never cease for want of themes, unless it be that the penury of language should compel our wonder to abide at home, since it cannot find garments in which to clothe its thoughts. When the soul is led by the Holy Spirit to take a clear view of Jesus in His various offices, how speedily the heart is on fire with love! To see Him stooping from His throne to become man, next yielding to suffering to become man's sympathising friend, and then bowing to death itself to become His Ransom, is enough to stir every passion of the soul. To discern Him by faith as the propitiation for sin, sprinkling His own blood within the veil, and nailing our sins to His cross, is a sight which never fails to excite the reverent, yet rapturous, admiration of the beholder. Who can behold the triumphs of the Prince of Peace, and not applaud Him? Who can know His illustrious merits, and not extol Him?

Doubtless this love of admiration is an after-thought, and can never be the primary acting of new-born love. The sailors rescued by the heroic daring of Grace Darling would first of all admire her as their deliverer, and afterwards, when they remembered her natural weakness, her philanthropic self-denial, her compassionate tenderness, and her heroic courage, they would give her their hearts for the manner in which the deed was done and the spirit which dictated it. In fact, apart from their own safety, they

could scarcely avoid paying homage to
the virtue which shone so gloriously in
her noble act. Never, throughout life,
could they forget their personal obligation
to that bravest of women; but at the
same time they would declare, that had it
not been their lot to have been rescued
from the depths, they could not have
refused their heart's admiration of a deed
so heroic, though they themselves had
not been profited by it. We, who are
saved by grace, have room enough in our
Redeemer's character for eternal love and
wonder. His characters are so varied,
and all of them so precious, that we may
still gaze and adore. The Shepherd fold-
ing the lambs in His bosom, the Breaker

dashing into pieces the opposing gates of brass, the Captain routing all His foes, the Brother born for adversity, and a thousand other delightful pictures of Jesus, are all calculated to stir the affections of the thoughtful Christian. It should be our endeavour to know more of Christ, that we may find more reasons for loving Him. A contemplation of the history, character, attributes, and offices of Jesus will often be the readiest way to renew our drooping love. The more clear is our view of Christ, the more complete will be our idea of Him ; and the more true our experience of Him, so much the more constant and unwavering will be our heart's hold of Him. Hence the importance of communion with Him, which is to a great extent the only means of knowing Him.

We would here caution the reader to make an important distinction when dwelling upon the phase of spiritual love now under consideration. Let him carefully remember that admiration of the moral character of Jesus of Nazareth may exist in an unregenerate heart, and that, apart from the love of gratitude, it is no acceptable fruit of the Spirit: so that this (in some senses) higher stone of the building, leans entirely upon the lower one, and without it is of no avail. Some pretend to admire the Prophet of Nazareth, but deny Him to be the Son of

God; others wonder at Him in His divine and human natures, but cannot lay hold on Him as their Redeemer; and many honour His perfect example, but despise His glorious sacrifice. Now, it is not love to a part of Christ which is the real work of the Spirit, but it is true devotion to the Christ of God in all that He is and does. Many manufacture a Christ of their own, and profess to love Him; but it is not respect to our own anointed, but to the Lord's Anointed, which can prove us to be God's elect. Seek then to know the Lord, that you may with your whole soul be united to Him in affection. Come, now, lay aside this volume for an hour and regale your-

self with a little of His company, then
will you join with the devout Hawker
in his oft-repeated confession :—" In
following Thee, Thou blessed Jesus,
every renewed discovery of Thee is
glorious, and every new attainment most
excellent. In Thy person, offices, character, and relations, Thou art most precious to my soul. Thou art a glorious
Redeemer, a glorious Head of Thy
Church and people ; a glorious Husband,
Brother, Friend, Prophet, Priest, and
King in Thy Zion. And when I behold
Thee in all these relative excellencies,
and can and do know Thee, and enjoy
Thee, and call Thee *mine* under every
one of them, surely I may well take up

the language of this sweet Scripture, and say, 'Thou art more glorious and excellent than all the mountains of Prey!'"*

If you are unable to obtain a view of the Man of grief and love, ask Him to reveal Himself by His Spirit, and when your prayer is heard your soul will speedily be ravished with delight.

"In manifested love explain
  Thy wonderful design ;
What meant the suffering Son of man,
  The streaming blood divine?

"Come Thou, and to my soul reveal
  The heights and depths of grace ;
The wounds which all my sorrows heal,
  That dear disfigured face :

* See his admirable " Portions."

" Before my eyes of faith confest
    Stand forth a slaughter'd Lamb ;
And wrap me in Thy crimson vest,
    And tell me all Thy name."

III. SYMPATHY WITH JESUS IN HIS GREAT DESIGN is a cause as well as an effect of love to Him. Sanctified men have an union of heart with Jesus, since their aims are common. Both are seeking to honour God, to uproot sin, to save souls, and extend the kingdom of God on earth. Though the saints are but the private soldiers, while Jesus is their glorious Leader, yet they are in the same army, and hence they have the same desire for victory. From this springs an increase of love ; for we cannot labour with and for those whom we esteem, without feeling ourselves more and more united to them. We love Jesus when we are advanced in the divine life, from a participation with Him in the great work of His incarnation. We long to see our fellow-men turned from darkness to light, and we love Him as the Sun of righteousness, who can alone illuminate them. We hate sin, and therefore we rejoice in Him as manifested to take away sin. We pant for holier and happier times, and therefore we adore Him as the coming Ruler of all lands, who will bring a millennium with Him in the day of His appearing. The more sincere our desires, and the more earnest

our efforts, to promote the glory of God
and the welfare of man, the more will our
love to Jesus increase. Idle Christians
always have lukewarm hearts, which are
at once the causes and effects of their
sloth. When the heart is fully engaged
in God's great work, it will glow with
love of the Great Son, who was Himself
a servant in the same great cause. Does
my philanthropy lead me to yearn over
dying men? Is my pity excited by their
miseries? Do I pray for their salvation,
and labour to be the means of it? Then
most assuredly I shall, for this very
reason, reverence and love the Friend of
sinners, the Saviour of the lost. Am I
so engrossed with the idea of God's

majesty, that my whole being pants to manifest His glory and extol His name? Then I shall most certainly cleave unto Him who glorified His Father, and in whose person all the attributes of Deity are magnified. If a sense of unity in aim be capable of binding hosts of men into one compact body, beating with one heart, and moving with the same step— then it is easy to believe that the heavenly object in which the saints and their Saviour are both united is strong enough to form a lasting bond of love between them.

Trusting that we may be enabled in our daily conduct to prove this truth, we pass on to another part of the subject.

IV. EXPERIENCE. Experience of the love, tenderness, and faithfulness of our Lord Jesus Christ will weld our hearts to Him. The very thought of the love of Jesus towards us is enough to inflame our holy passions, but experience of it heats the furnace seven times hotter. He has been with us in our trials, cheering and consoling us, sympathising with every groan, and regarding every tear with affectionate compassion. Do we not love Him for this? He has befriended us in every time of need, so bounteously supplying all our wants out of the riches of His fulness, that He has not suffered us to lack any good thing. Shall we be unmindful of such unwearying care? He has helped us in every difficulty, furnishing us with strength equal to our day; He has levelled the mountains before us, and filled up the valleys; He has made rough places plain, and crooked things straight. Do we not love Him for this also? In all our doubts He has directed us in the path of wisdom, and led us in the way of knowledge. He has not suffered us to wander; He has led us by a right way through the pathless wilderness. Shall we not praise Him for this? He has repelled our enemies, covered our heads in the day of battle, broken the teeth of the oppressor, and made us more than conquerors. Can we forget such mighty grace? When our sins have broken our peace, stained our garments, and pierced us with many sorrows, He has restored our souls, and led us in the path of righteousness for His name's sake. Are we not constrained to call upon all that is within us to bless His holy name? He has been as good as His word; not one promise has been broken, but all have come to pass. In no single instance has He failed us; He has never been unkind, unmindful, or unwise. The harshest strokes of His providence have been as full of love as the softest embraces of His condescending fellowship. We cannot,—we dare not—find fault with Him. He hath done all things well. There is no flaw in His behaviour, no suspicion upon His affection. His love is indeed that perfect love which casteth out fear ; the review of it is sweet to contemplate ; the very remembrance of it is like ointment poured forth, and the present enjoyment of it, the experience of it at the present moment, is beyond all things delightful. Whatever may be our present position, it has in it peculiarities unknown to any other state, and hence it affords special grounds of love. Are we on the mountains ? We bless Him that He maketh our feet like hind's feet, and maketh us to stand upon our high places. Are we in the valley ? Then we praise Him that His rod and staff do comfort us. Are we in sickness ? We love Him for His gracious visitations. If we be in health, we bless Him for His merciful preservations. At home or abroad, on the land or the sea, in health or sickness, in poverty or wealth, Jesus, the never-failing Friend, affords us tokens of His grace, and binds our hearts to Him in the bonds of constraining gratitude.

It must, however, be confessed that all the saints do not profit from their experience in an equal measure, and none of them so much as they might. All the experience of a Christian is not Christian experience. Much of our time is occupied with exercises as unprofitable as they are unpleasant. The progress of a traveller must not be measured by the amount of his toil, unless we can obtain a satisfactory proof that all his toil was expended in the right path ; for let him journey ever so swiftly, if his path be full of wanderings, he will gain but little by his labours. When we follow on to know the Lord in His own appointed way, the promise assures us that we shall attain to knowledge ; but if we run in the way of our own devising, we need not wonder if we find ourselves surrounded with darkness instead of light. However, the Lord, who graciously overrules evil for good, has been pleased to permit it to remain as a rule in the lives of His children, that they learn by experience,—and sure we are that, were we not dull scholars, we

should in the experience of a single day
discover a thousand reasons for loving the
Redeemer.   The most barren day in all
our years blossoms with remembrances
of His loving-kindness, while the more
memorable seasons yield a hundredfold
the fruits of His goodness.   Though some
days may add but little to the heap, yet by
little and little it increases to a mountain.
Little experiences, if well husbanded, will
soon make us rich in love.   Though the
banks of the river do shelve but gently,
yet he that is up to the ankles shall find
the water covering his knees, if he do but
continue his wading.   Blessed is the saint
whose love to his Lord hath become con-
firmed with his years, so that his heart is

fixed, and fired, and flaming. He with his grey hairs and venerable countenance commands the attention of all men when he speaks well of the Lord Jesus, whom he hath tried and proved through more than half a century of tribulation mingled with rejoicing. As a youth his love was true, but we thought it little more than a momentary flash, which would die as hastily as it was born ; but now no man can doubt its sincerity, for it is a steady flame, like the burning of a well-trimmed lamp. Experience, when blessed by the Holy Spirit, is the saint's daily income, by which he getteth rich in affection ; and he who hath for a long time amassed his portion of treasure may well be conceived to be more rich therein than the young beginner, who has as yet received but little. Would to God that we were all more careful to obtain and retain the precious gems which lie at our feet in our daily experience !

The experienced believer is in advance of his younger brethren if his experience has developed itself in a deeper, steadier, and more abiding love of Christ. He is to the babe in grace what the oak is to the sapling—more firmly rooted, more strong in heart, and broader in his spread ; his love, too, is to the affection of the beginner what the deep-rolling river is to the sparkling rill. Especially is this the case if he has done business on great waters, and has been buried beneath the billows of affliction. He will, if he have passed through such exercises, be a mighty witness of the worthiness of his Lord,—for tribulation unfolds the delights of covenant engagements, and drives the soul to feed upon them. It cuts away every other prop, and compels the soul to test the solidity of the pillar of divine faithfulness; it throws a cloud over the face of all created good, and leads the spirit to behold the sacred beauties of the Son of man; and thus it enables the believer to know in the most certain manner the all-sufficiency of the grace of the Lord Jesus. Tried saints are constrained to love their Redeemer; not only on ac-

count of deliverance out of trouble, but
also because of that sweet comfort which
He affords them whilst they are enduring
the cross. They have found adversity to
be a wine-press, in which the juice of
the grapes of Eschol could be trodden
out ; an olive-press, to extract the precious oil from the gracious promises.
Christ is the honey-comb, but experience
must suck forth the luscious drops ; He
is frankincense, but fiery trials must burn
out the perfume ; He is a box of spike-
nard, but the hard hand of trouble must
break the box and pour forth the ointment. When this is done, when Jesus
is experimentally known, He is loved in
a higher manner than the newborn Chris-

tian can aspire to talk of. Aged and mellow saints have so sweet a savour of Christ in them that their conversation is like streams from Lebanon, sweetly refreshing to him who delights to hear of the glories of redeeming love. They have tried the anchor in the hour of storm, they have tested the armour in the day of battle, they have proved the shadow of the great rock in the burning noontide in the weary land ; therefore do they talk of these things, and of *Him* who is all these unto them, with an unction and a relish which we, who have but just put on our harness, can enjoy, although we cannot attain unto it at present. We must dive into the same waters if we would bring up the same pearls. May the great Illuminator sow our path with light, that we may increase in knowledge of the love *of* Christ, and in earnestness of love *to* Christ, in proportion as we draw near to the celestial city.

We now advance to another step, which stands in strict connection with the subject upon which we have just meditated.

V. COMMUNION opens up another means by which love is excited, and its nature affected. We love Him because we have seen Him, and entered into fellowship with Him. However true and faithful the tidings which another person may bring us concerning the Saviour, we shall never feel love towards Him in all the power of it until we have with our own eyes beheld Him, or, rather, have laid hold on Him with our own faith. Personal intercourse with Jesus is pre-eminently a cause of love, and it so infallibly quickens the affections that it is impossible to live in the society of Jesus without loving Him. Nearness of life towards the Lamb will necessarily involve greatness of love to Him. As nearness to the sun increases the temperature of the various planets, so close communion with Jesus raises the heat of the affections towards Him.

We hope to have another opportunity

of unfolding the sweetness of communion, and therefore we will but notice one part of it—viz., Christ's manifestations, as being a mighty incentive to affection. Our blessed Lord, at intervals more or less frequent, is graciously pleased to shed abroad in the soul a most enchanting and rapturous sense of His love. He opens the ear of the favoured saint to hear the sweet canticles of the Bridegroom's joy, and softly He singeth His song of loves. He manifests His heart to the heart of His chosen ones, so that they know Him to be the sweetest, firmest, and most ardent of lovers. They feel that He loves as a head, as a father, as a friend, as a kinsman, as a brother, as a husband; they behold the love of all relationships united and exceeded in the love of Christ. They are confident that He loves them more than they love themselves; yea, that He loves them above His own life. This tends to raise their souls towards Him; He becomes wholly delectable unto them, and is enshrined upon the highest throne of their hearts. Possessed with a sense of the love of their dying Lord, they feel that had they a heart as wide as eternity, it could not contain more love than they desire to give Him. Thus are they impelled to daring service and patient suffering for His sake. "There is a power in this love which conquers, captivates, and overpowers the man, so that he cannot but love. God's love hath a generative power; our love is brought forth by His love." * Say, poor soul, what get you in Christ whenever you go to Him? Can you not say, "Oh! I get more love to Him than I had before; I never approached near to Him but I gained a large draught and ample fill of love to God"? Out of His fulness we receive grace for grace, and love for love. In a word, by faith we behold the glory of the Lord as in a glass, and are changed into the same image—and the image of God is love. No way so ready

---

* R. Erskine.

for begetting love *to* Christ as a sense of the love *of* Christ. The one is a load-stone to attract the other. As fire grows by the addition of fuel, so does our love to Christ increase by renewed and en-larged discoveries of His love to us. Love is love's food. If, as parents, we make known our love to our children, and deal wisely with them, it is but natural that their affections should become more and more knit to us; so it seems but as in the common course of things that where much of divine love is perceived by the soul, there will be a return of affection in some degree proportionate to the measure of the manifestation. As we pour water into a dry pump when we desire to obtain

more, so must we have the love of Christ
imparted to the heart before we shall feel
any uprisings of delight in Him.   Hence
the importance of the apostolic prayer,
that we may be able to understand with
all saints what is the breadth, and length,
and depth, and height, and to know the
love of Christ, which passeth knowledge.
Beloved fellow-Christian, pray for more
open discoveries of the love and loveli-
ness of Christ, and thus shall thy languid
passions move more readily in the paths
of obedience.   We have all too much
cause to mourn the poverty of our love ;
let us not be slow to seek the help of the
God of Israel to enable us to profit by
all the condescending manifestations with

which the Lord sees fit to favour us.

VI. LOVE TO THE PERSON OF JESUS is a most delightful state of divine life. It will be observed that the Song of the Spouse, which is doubtless intended to be the expression of the highest order of love, is composed rather of descriptions of the *person* of the Bridegroom than of any relation of the deeds which He performed. The whole language of the Book of Canticles is love, but its most overflowing utterances are poured forth upon the sacred *person* of the Well-Beloved. How do the words succeed each other in marvellous and melodious

succession when the Church pours forth
the fulness of its heart in praises of His
beauties !—" My Beloved is white and
ruddy, the chiefest among ten thousand.
His head is as the most fine gold, His
locks are bushy, and black as a raven.
His eyes are as the eyes of doves by the
rivers of waters, washed with milk, and
fitly set. His cheeks are as a bed of
spices, as sweet flowers. His lips like
lilies, dropping sweet smelling myrrh.
His hands are as gold rings set with the
beryl : His belly is as bright ivory over-
laid with sapphires. His legs are as
pillars of marble, set upon sockets of fine
gold : His countenance is as Lebanon,
excellent as the cedars. His mouth is

most sweet: yea, He is altogether lovely."*
Here it is not the crown, but the *head*,
which is the theme of song; not the
garment, but the unrobed body; not the
shoes, but the feet. The song does not
celebrate His descent from the King of
ages, nor His lordship over the ministers
of fire, nor His perpetual priesthood, nor
His unbounded sovereignty; but it finds
music enough in His lips, and beauty
sufficient in His eyes without the glories
which His high offices and omnipotent
grace have procured for Him. This indeed is true love; though the wife regards
her husband's gifts, and honours his rank

---

* Sol. Song v. 10-16.

and titles, yet she sets her affection upon his person, loves *him* better than his gifts, and esteems him for his own sake rather than for his position among men. Let us here observe, lest we should be misunderstood, that we do not for a moment intend to insinuate that in the earlier states of the sacred grace of love, there is any lack of love *to His person.* We know that the first gushing of the fount of love is to *Christ,* and at all times the soul goes out towards *Him;* but we make a distinction which we think will be readily perceived, between love to the person, for the sake of benefits received and offices performed, and love to the person *for the person's sake.* To suppose that a believer loves the office apart from the person is to suppose an absurdity; but to say that he may love the person apart from the office is but to declare a great fact. We love *Him* at all times, but only the heavenly-minded love Him *for His own person's sake.*

What a precious subject for contemplation is the glorious being who is called Emmanuel, God with us, and yet "the I am," "God over all"! The complex person of the Mediator, Jesus Christ, is the centre of a believer's heart. He adores Him in all the attributes of His God-head as very God of very God—Eternal, Infinite, Almighty, Immutable. He bows before Him as "God over all, blessed for ever,"

and pays Him loving homage as the
everlasting Father, the Prince of peace;
and at the same time he delights to consider Him as the infant of Bethlehem,
the Man of sorrows, the Son of man,
bone of our bone and flesh of our flesh,
tempted in all points like as we are, and
owning kindred with the children of men.
As man yet God, creature yet Creator,
infant and Infinite, despised yet exalted,
scourged though Omnipotent, dying yet
eternal,—our dear Redeemer must ever
be the object of wondering affection.
Yea, when faith is dim and the Christian
is in doubt as to his possession of his
Lord, he will at times be able to feel that
his thoughts of his Master's person are

as high as ever. "Though He slay me,
I must love Him. If He will not look
upon me, I cannot but bless Him still.
He is good and glorious, even though He
damn me for ever. I must speak well of
Him, even if He will not permit me to
hope in His mercy; for He is a glorious
Christ, and I will not deny it, though He
should now shut up His bowels against
an unworthy creature like myself." This
is the sentiment of the quickened child
of God, when his heart is thoroughly
occupied with a full and faithful view of
his divine Lord.

Oh, the savour of the name of Jesus,
when heard by the ear which has been
opened by the Spirit! Oh, the beauty

of the person of Jesus, when seen with the eye of faith by the illumination of the Holy One of Israel! As the light of the morning, when the sun ariseth, "as a morning without clouds," is our Well-Beloved unto us. The sight of the burning bush made Moses put off his shoes, but the transporting vision of Jesus makes us put off all the world. When once He is seen we can discern no beauties in all the creatures in the universe. He, like the sun, hath absorbed all other glories into His own excessive brightness. This is the pomegranate which love feeds upon, the flagon wherewith it is comforted. A sight of Jesus causes such union of heart with Him, such goings out of the affections after Him, and such meltings of the spirit towards Him, that its expressions often appear to carnal men to be extravagant and forced, when they are nothing but the free, unstudied, and honest effusions of its love. Hence it is that the Song of Solomon has been so frequently assailed, and has had its right to a place in the canon so fiercely disputed. The same critics would deny the piety of Rutherford, or the reverence of Herbert. They are themselves ignorant of the divine passion of love to Jesus, and therefore the language of the enraptured heart is unintelligible to them. They are poor translators of love's celestial tongue who think it to be at all allied with the amorous superfluities

uttered by carnal passions. Jesus is the
only one upon whom the loving believer
has fixed his eye, and in his converse
with his Lord he will often express himself in language which is meant only for
his Master's ear, and which worldlings
would utterly contemn could they but listen
to it.   Nevertheless love, like wisdom, is
" justified of her children."

Heaven itself, although it be a fertile
land, flowing with milk and honey, can
produce no fairer flower than the Rose
of Sharon; its highest joys mount no
higher than the head of Jesus; its sweetest
bliss is found in His name alone.   If we
would know heaven, let us know Jesus;
if we would be heavenly, let us love Jesus.

Oh, that we were perpetually in His company, that our hearts might ever be satisfied with His love! Let the young believer seek after a clear view of the person of Jesus, and then let him implore the kindling fire of the Holy Spirit to light up his whole soul with fervent affection. Love to Jesus is the basis of all true piety, and the intensity of this love will ever be the measure of our zeal for His glory. Let us love Him with all our hearts, and then diligent labour and consistent conversation will be sure to follow.

VII. RELATIONSHIP TO CHRIST, when fully felt and realised, produces a peculiar warmth of affection towards Him. The

Holy Spirit is pleased, at certain favoured seasons, to open up to the understanding and reveal to the affections the nearness of Jesus to the soul. At one time we are blessed with a delightful sense of *brother-hood* with Christ. "The Man is thy near Kinsman" sounds like news from a far country. "In ties of blood with sinners one" rings in our ears like the music of Sabbath bells. We had said, like the spouse, "Oh that Thou wert as my Brother!" and lo! the wish is gratified. He stands before us in all His con-descenion, and declares He is not ashamed to call us brethren. Unveiling His face, He reveals Himself as the Son of man, our Kinsman near allied by blood. He manifests Himself to our rejoicing spirit as "the first-born among many brethren," and He reminds us that we are "joint-heirs with Him," although He is "Heir of all things." The fraternity of Jesus cannot fail to quicken us to the most ardent affection, and when He Himself thus confesses the relationship, our soul is melted at His speech. That sweet name "Brother" is like perfume to the believer, and when he lays hold upon it, it imparts its fragrance to him. We have sometimes had such a sense of satisfaction in meditation upon this heavenly doctrine, that we counted all the honours and glories of this world to be but loss compared with the excellency of it. For this one fact of brotherhood with Christ we could have bartered crowns and empires, and have laughed at the worldly barterer as a fool, infinitely more mad than Esau when he took a pitiful mess of pottage as the purchase-price of a mighty birthright. God the Holy Ghost has made the fulness of the doctrine of the relationship of Jesus roll into our soul like a river, and we have been entirely carried away in its wondrous torrent. Our thoughts have been entirely absorbed in the one transcendently glorious idea of brotherhood with Jesus, and then the emotions have arisen with great vehemence, and we have pressed *Him* to our bosom, have wept for joy upon His shoulder, and have lost ourselves in adoring love of Him who thus discovered Himself as bone of our bone, and flesh of our flesh. We feel we must love our Brother; even nature joins her voice with grace to claim the entire heart; and verily, in seasons of such gracious manifestations, the claim is fully met, and the right gladly acknowledged.

Another delightful relationship of the Lord Jesus is that of Husband, and here He is indeed to be beloved. Young Christians are married to Christ, but they have not in most cases realised the gracious privilege; but the more enlightened believer rejoices in the remembrance of the marriage union of Christ and His spouse. To him the affection, protection, provision, honour, and intimacy involved in the divine nuptials of the blessed Jesus with His elect are well-springs of constant joy. "Thy Maker is thy Husband" is to him a choice portion of the Word, and he feasts upon it day and night, when the gracious Spirit is pleased to enable him to lay hold upon it by faith. A tranquil, confident frame will immediately result from a satisfactory persuasion of this glorious truth, and with it there will be a fervency of affection and a continued union of heart to Christ Jesus, which is hardly attainable in any other manner.

In His conjugal relation to His Church,

the Lord Jesus takes great delight, and desires that we should see the glory of it. He would have us consider Him in the act of betrothing and espousing His Church unto Himself: "Go forth," saith He, "O ye daughters of Jerusalem, and behold King Solomon with the crown wherewith his mother crowned him in the day of his espousals, and in the day of the gladness of his heart." *

"It is the gladness of the heart of Christ, and the joy of His soul, to take poor sinners into relation with Himself;" † and if so, it cannot fail to be an

---

* Sol. Song iii. 11.

† Owen.

equal source of rejoicing to those who are thus favoured. Meditate much on thy divine relationships, and thine heart shall be much warmed thereby.

VIII. A persuasion of our UNION to Jesus must also stir up the passions to a holy flame. We are, by the decree of God, made one with our Covenant Head, the Lord Jesus. From before all worlds this eternal union was most firmly settled upon a substantial basis; but our personal knowledge of it is a thing of time, and is vouchsafed to us in the appointed season by God the Holy Ghost. How swiftly doth the heart pursue its Lord when it has learned its *oneness* to Him! What man will not love his own flesh? Who will not love himself? Now, when the soul perceives the indissoluble union which exists between itself and the Saviour, it can no more resist the impulse of affection than a man can forbear to love his own body. It is doubtless a high attainment in the divine life to be fully possessed with a sense of vital union to Christ, and hence the love arising from it is of a peculiarly rich and vehement character. Some pastures give richness to the flesh of the cattle which feed upon them: truly, this is a fat pasture, and the affection which feedeth upon it cannot be otherwise than excellent to a superlative degree. In fine, as an abiding sense of oneness with the Lord is one of the sweetest works of the Spirit in the souls of the elect, so the love springing therefrom is of the very highest and most spiritual nature. None can surpass it; yea, it is questionable whether so high a degree of affection can be attained by any other means, however forcible and inflaming. But set it down as a rule that we ought never to halt or sit down in any attainment of nearness to Jesus until we have brought it to such a measure that no more can be enjoyed, and until we have reached the utmost possible height therein. If there be an inner chamber in which the King doth store His choicest fruits, let us enter, for

He bids us make free with all in His house; and if there be a secret place where He doth show His loves, let us hasten thither and embrace Him whom our soul loveth, and there let us abide until we see Him face to face in the upper skies.

But what will be the love of Heaven? Here we utterly fail in description or conception. The best enjoyments of Christ on earth are but as the dipping our finger in water for the cooling of our thirst; but heaven is bathing in seas of bliss: even so our love here is but one drop of the same substance as the waters of the ocean, but not comparable for magnitude or depth. Oh, how sweet it will be to be married to the Lord Jesus, and to enjoy for ever, and without any interruption, the heavenly delights of His society! Surely, if a glimpse of Him melteth our soul, the full fruition of Him will be enough to burn us up with affec-tion. It is well that we shall have more noble frames in heaven than we have here, otherwise we should die of love in the very land of life. An honoured saint was once so ravished with a revelation of his Lord's love, that feeling his mortal frame to be unable to sustain more of such bliss, he cried, "Hold, Lord; it is enough, it is enough!" But there we shall be able to set the bottomless well of love to our lips, and drink on for ever, and yet feel no weakness. Ah, that will be love indeed which shall overflow our souls for ever in our Father's house above! Who can tell the transports, the raptures, the amazements of delight which that love shall beget in us? and who can guess the sweetness of the song, or the swiftness of the obedience which will be the heavenly expressions of love made perfect? No heart can conceive the surpassing bliss which the saints shall enjoy when the sea of their love to Christ, and the ocean of Christ's love to them, shall meet each other, and raise a very tempest of delight. The distant prospect is full of joy: what must be the fruition of it? To answer that question we must wait all the days of our appointed time till our change come, unless the Lord Himself should suddenly appear in the clouds to glorify us with Himself throughout eternity.

Beloved fellow-heirs of the same inheritance, we have thus reviewed some of the causes and phases of the Christian grace of love ; let us now ask ourselves the question, How is it with your love ? Is it hot or cold ? Is it decaying or increasing ? How stands the heart, God-ward and Christ-ward ? Is it not far too slow in its motions, too chilly in its devotion ? We must admit it is so. Let us use the various arguments of this chapter as levers for lifting our heavy hearts to greater heights of affection, and then let us unitedly cry,—

" Come, Holy Spirit, heavenly Dove,
     With all Thy quickening powers ;
Come, shed abroad the Saviour's love,
     And that shall kindle ours."

It may be that the sneering critic has been offended with all this discourse concerning love, and has turned upon his heel, protesting with vehemence that he is of a philosophic spirit, and will never endure such sickly sentimentalism. To him religion is thought, not emotion. It is a cold, speculative, unfeeling divinity which he believes, and its effects upon his mind are the reverse of enthusiastic.

Reason, "heavenly Reason," is his God, and Feeling must lie dormant beneath the throne of his great deity. We beg to remind him that the religion of the cross was intended to stir the soul with deep emotion, and that where it is truly received it accomplishes its end ; but that if the passions be not moved by it, there is a strong presumption that it has never been in true operation. We do not wonder that, to the man who views religion as a mere compendium of truths for the head, it is a powerless thing, for it is intended to work in another manner. Wine may serve to cheer the heart, but who would expect to feel its exhilarating influence

by pouring it upon his head? The holy
Gospel makes its first appeal to man's
heart, and until it be heard in that secret
chamber it is not heard at all. So long
as mere reason is the only listener, the
melody of the cross will be unheard.
Charm we never so wisely, men cannot
hear the music until the ears of the heart
are opened. Vinet * has thus expressed
himself upon this subject:—" Ah! how
can reason, cold reason, comprehend
such a thing as the substitution of the
innocent for the guilty; as the compassion which reveals itself in severity of
punishment in that shedding of blood,

---

* See his " Vital Christianity."

without which, it is said, there can be
no expiation? It will not make, I dare
affirm, a single step towards the knowledge of that divine mystery, until, càst-
ing away its ungrateful speculations, it
yields to a stronger power the task of
terminating the difficulty. That power is
the heart, which fixes itself entirely on
the love that shines forth in the work of
redemption; cleaves without distraction
to the sacrifice of the adorable victim;
lets the natural impression of that un-
paralleled love penetrate freely, and
develop itself gradually in its interior.
Oh, how quickly, then, are the veils torn
away, and the shadows dissipated for
ever! How little difficulty does he who

loves find in comprehending love!" To the heart all divine mysteries are but simplicities, and when reason is measuring the apparently inaccessible heights, love is already shouting on the summit. Let the cold, calculating worshipper of intellect reserve his sneers for himself. Experience is one of the highest of sciences, and the emotions claim a high precedence in the experience which is from God. That which these boasters contemn as an old wives' story is not one half so contemptible as themselves —yea, more, the pious feelings at which they jeer are as much beyond their highest thoughts as the sonnets of angels excel the gruntings of swine.

It has become fashionable to allow the title of " intellectual preachers " to a class of men whose passionless essays are combinations of metaphysical quibbles and heretical doctrines ; who are shocked at the man who excites his hearers beyond the freezing-point of insensibility, and are quite elated if they hear that their homily could only be understood by a few. It is, however, no question whether these men deserve their distinctive title ; it may be settled as an axiom that falsehood is no intellectual feat, and that unintelligible jargon is no evidence of a cultured mind. There must be in our religion a fair proportion of believing, thinking, understanding, and discerning, but there must be also the preponderating influences of feeling, loving, delighting, and desiring. That religion is worth nothing which has no dwelling in man but his brain. To love much is to be wise; to grow in affection is to grow in knowledge, and to increase in tender attachment is to be making high proficiency in divine things.

Look to thy love, O Christian! and let the carnal revile thee never so much do thou persevere in seeking to walk with Christ, to feel His love, and triumph in His grace.

TO THE UNCONVERTED READER

FRIEND,—This time we will not preach the terrors of the law to thee, although they are thy deserts. We wish thee well, and if threatening will not awaken thee, we will try what wooing may accomplish, and oh! may the Holy Spirit bless the means to thy soul's salvation.

The Lord Jesus hath purchased unto Himself a number beyond all human count, and we would have thee mark who and what they were by nature.

The blood-bought ones, before their regeneration, were in the gall of bitterness and in the bonds of iniquity; they were aliens from the commonwealth of Israel, and strangers from the covenants of promise; they had chosen to themselves other gods, and were joined to idols; they walked according to the course of this world, according to the Prince of the power of the air, the spirit that now worketh in the children of disobedience; they were polluted in their blood, cast out in the open field to perish; they were despisers of God, in league with hell, and in covenant with Death; but nevertheless they were chosen, were redeemed, and have received the glorious title of Sons and Daughters.

Now, Friend, if free grace has done thus with one and another, why should it

not accomplish the same for thee? Dost
thou feel thy deep necessities? Do thy
bowels yearn for mercy? Art thou made
willing to be saved in God's way? Then
be of good cheer. The promise is thine,
the blood of Jesus was shed for thee, the
Holy Spirit is at work with thee, thy
salvation draweth nigh. *He that calleth
upon the name of the Lord shall be saved.*
Thy cries shall yet be heard, since they
come from a broken heart and a contrite
spirit. Remember, faith in Jesus alone
can give thee peace.

But art thou still hard and stolid, still
brutish and worldly? Then, permit the
writer to weep over thee, and bring thy
case before the Lord his God. Oh, that

the Lord would melt thee by the fire of
His word ! Oh, that He would break thee
with His hammer, and humble thee at
His feet ! Alas for thee, unless this be
done ! Oh, that omnipotent grace would
snatch thee from the ruin of the proud,
and deliver thy feet from going down into
the pit ! Miserable man ! a brother's
heart longeth after thee, and fain would
see thee saved. Oh, why art thou so
indifferent to thyself when others can
scarce refrain from tears on thy behalf !
By thy mother's prayers, thy sister's tears
and thy father's anxieties, I beseech thee
give a reason for thy sottish indifference
to thine eternal welfare. Dost thou now
come to thyself ? Dost thou now exclaim,

"I will arise and go unto my Father"?
Oh, be assured of a welcome reception,
of gladsome entertainment, and loving
acceptance!